SCIENTIFICALLY ENGINEERED FOODS

The Debate Over What's on Your Plate

With genetic engineering, scientists can create plants that will produce their own pesticides.

SCIENTIFICALLY ENGINEERED FOODS

The Debate Over What's on Your Plate

Allan B. Cobb

The Rosen Publishing Group, Inc.
New York

Published in 2000, 2003 by The Rosen Publishing Group, Inc.

29 East 21st Street, New York, NY 10010

2003260

Revised Edition 2003

Library of Congress Cataloging-in-Publication Data

Cobb, Allan B.

Scientifically engineered foods: the debate over what's on your plate/Allan B. Cobb—2nd. ed.

    p. cm.—(Focus on science and society)

Includes bibliographical references and index.

ISBN 0-8239-4090-X

1. Food—Biotechnology. 2. Crops—Genetic engineering. 3. Food—Biotechnology—Social aspects. 4. Crops—Genetic engineering—Social aspects. 5. Food—Biotechnology—Safety measures. 6. Crops—Genetic engineering—Safety measures.

I. Title. II. Series.

TP248.65.F66 C63 2000

631.5'233—dc21

                                                  00-020583

Manufactured in the United States of America

CONTENTS

Genetic engineering sounds miraculous, but serious health and environmental concerns need to be addressed.

INTRODUCTION

Imagine fruits and vegetables shaped like cubes. Imagine that the fruits and vegetables stay fresh longer than all others. Farmers would like these fruits and veggies because they could be packed in crates with little wasted space. The farmer would not have to rush to get the products to market before they spoil because they stay fresh so long. This would make shipping easier, less costly, and less stressful. Then imagine that a plant exists that can release pesticides to kill any insects that are attacking it. Wouldn't life be simpler with these kinds of possibilities?

Well, though scientists haven't figured out how to make cubic fruits and vegetables, they have created plants that produce their own pesticides. Scientists do this by inserting genetic material from another organism into the DNA of crops. This is a process known as genetic engineering, or GE. Things that are made through genetic engineering are also known as GE products.

SCIENTIFICALLY ENGINEERED FOODS

Genetic engineering has found its way into the foods that we eat. Genetically engineered or modified foods have been on the market since the early 1990s. Genetically engineered crops, fruits, and veggies are not scary or demonic looking. What does a GE veggie, such as a GE tomato, look like? It looks just like any other tomato you might see at the grocery store. Scientists have genetically engineered soybeans so that they have more protein than regular soybeans. If you visually compared a normal soybean with a genetically engineered one, you probably couldn't tell the difference.

GE foods were not placed on the market without controversy. For some people, genetic engineering conjures up images of Frankenstein-like creatures and bizarre creations. Some people think that GE products are unnatural. This is because genetic engineering does what nature cannot.

Timeline

1700s	1840s	1900s	1950s	1970s	1980s
Scientists begin to cross-pollinate plants to make hybrids. The hybrids have beneficial characteristics of both original plants.	Gregor Mendel's studies of pea plants are the start of modern genetic research. They lead to the use of genetics to predict the characteristics of offspring.	European scientists use Mendel's Law to breed improved plants. This starts the modern selective breeding movement.	The first plant is regenerated entirely in a laboratory. In 1953, James Watson and Francis Crick develop the first model of DNA, determining its structure and how it transfers genetic information.	Seedless fruits are bred. Scientists learn to "read" genetic information and identify specific genes that have unique functions.	Scientists discover how to transfer genes from one organism to another. The science of genetic engineering is born.

INTRODUCTION

Some consumers and scientists wonder whether GE products and foods are safe. The long-term effects of GE products have not been established yet. Some people worry that new toxins or poisons will be produced from the GE products. Some people believe that GE plants and food products will affect the environment in harmful ways. This book explores some of the issues and ethical questions that are raised by those concerned about scientifically altering the foods we eat, the crops we grow, and the livestock we feed and take care of.

1983	1985	1987	1990	1994	1998	2002
Tobacco becomes the first transgenic crop plant. Scientists give the plant a gene for resisting an antibiotic.	Plants genetically engineered to resist pests are field-tested.	Scientists create transgenic potatoes and soybeans.	Genetically engineered cotton is field-tested. Scientists also create the first transgenic corn.	The Flavr Savr tomato is approved by the FDA for sale in the United States.	Of all corn grown in the United States, 32 percent is from transgenic plants.	GE crops reach 130 million acres worldwide.

CHAPTER 1

WHAT ARE SCIENTIFICALLY ENGINEERED FOODS?

Scientifically engineered foods are plants and animals that scientists have changed in the laboratory. There are a number of methods—including GE—that scientists use to alter foods in the laboratory. Why would scientists change plants and animals? There are a number of answers to this question. The scientifically engineered plants may resist disease, resist freezing, grow faster, and produce more food. Scientifically engineered foods and plants can contain different and helpful proteins that their counterparts found in nature do not contain. Scientifically engineered animals may gain weight faster, resist disease, or grow larger more quickly than normal.

When people speak of scientifically engineered foods, they are referring to a number of different ways scientists change plants and animals. The most common method of scientifically engineering foods is the modification or alteration of the genetic structure, or DNA, of a plant or animal.

11

SCIENTIFICALLY ENGINEERED FOODS

By altering an organism's DNA, we can change the traits of that organism. Traits include color, size, shape, health, and growth. Traits are also known as characteristics. The scientific engineering method that alters DNA and traits of an organism is GE, or genetic engineering. Scientists alter or add genetic material to the cells of a plant, animal, or organism to produce a desired trait.

Selective breeding has been used to develop specific characteristics in dogs.

Breeding

Breeding has been used for thousands of years to change the traits of organisms. In the past, breeding was usually done by farmers, ranchers, or scientists. Breeding was done to improve the traits of plants and animals. If a particular type of plant grew in poor soil but its fruit tasted bad, a farmer would try to breed that plant with another plant that had great-tasting fruit. Breeding the two plants would create a new plant. The new plant would be able to grow in any type of soil, even poor soil. It would also have great-tasting fruit. The new plant would have the desirable traits of the original two plants—the ability to grow in poor soil and great-tasting fruit.

Think about all the different breeds of dogs. They range from the small Chihuahua to the large Great Dane. Dogs were selected for specific traits and then bred with other dogs with similar traits. This led to the variety of breeds seen today. Some, like the golden retriever, were bred for hunting. Others, like the husky, were bred to pull sleds. Even though the dogs all look different, they are all the same species.

These same selective breeding principles have been applied to many other animals, including cows, horses, sheep, goats, and chickens. Selective breeding of plants brought about different varieties of corn, squash, tomatoes, carrots, and onions. Plants are usually bred to produce large, tasty edible parts that are resistant to disease.

Farming animals—such as cows, pigs, chickens, and geese—have undergone selective breeding for as long as humans have been farming and ranching. Selective breeding is a slow process. It may take many breeding attempts and many generations of animals or plants before the desired traits are achieved. Today, scientists can obtain the results of selective breeding in a much shorter period of time. By manipulating DNA, scientists can create the desired traits in only one generation of plants or animals.

Scientists manipulate DNA using techniques such as recombinant DNA. This technology allows scientists to go beyond the bounds of traditional breeding. Using recombinant DNA, scientists can actually insert genetic material from different organisms (plants or animals) into the DNA of other plants or animals. For example, scientists can insert genetic material from a cow into a corn plant. This results in genetically engineered corn.

Genetic Engineering

Genetically engineered organisms have new DNA, or DNA that has been changed from its original state. The new DNA is the combination of the original DNA and the new section of DNA that was inserted from another plant or animal. When the organism reproduces, or mates, the new DNA is passed to offspring. A plant, animal, or organism that has received inserted DNA is called a transgenic plant, animal, or organism. Transgenic plants, animals, and organisms still function as their counterparts found in nature, but they also have a few new traits that may add to their functions or purpose.

Genetic engineering of food, plants, and animals is done to make certain processes easier. Examples of things made easier by GE include food processes and pharmaceutical processes.

Food Process

One of the first uses for genetically engineered organisms was in the cheese industry. An enzyme called rennin is used to make cheese. Rennin was originally extracted (taken) from the stomachs of unweaned calves. Unweaned calves are baby cows that still drink their mothers' milk. The process of extracting the enzyme was slow and it produced minimal amounts, so the price of rennin was high.

In 1990, the Food and Drug Administration (FDA) approved a new process for making rennin. Scientists used recombinant DNA technology to sidestep the use of calves. The DNA that is responsible for producing the enzymes in a calf's stomach was copied from a calf's cells. The DNA was put into bacteria. The bacteria with the new DNA began to produce rennin. This rennin is exactly the same as rennin from a calf, except that it comes from bacteria. Large amounts of bacteria can produce the enzyme in greater amounts. The result is a cheap source of rennin for making cheese. According to the Public Broadcasting Service (PBS), about 90 percent of all cheese is made using these GE enzymes.

Pharmaceutical Process

According to PBS, about 200 million people worldwide have benefited from genetically engineered pharmaceuticals. GE has made the production of pharmaceutical drugs easier. It has made it easier to make important and rare ingredients for drugs. These drugs help treat diseases and conditions such as growth deficiency and diabetes.

The human growth hormone—also known as HGH— is responsible for a person's growth. Some children suffer from human growth hormone deficiency. This is a condition where there is not enough of the hormone to allow normal growth. Children with the deficiency are given extra amounts of HGH to help them grow. Before GE, the human growth hormone was obtained from the pituitary glands of corpses, or deceased people. Now the gene that is responsible for making HGH can be copied over and over again. The DNA is inserted into bacteria or other organisms. The bacteria begin to produce HGH. This means that corpses are no longer needed. It also provides a much easier and less expensive way to get the growth hormone.

Diabetes patients are treated with insulin. Before GE, insulin was made by using the pancreases of pigs. Many diabetics had allergies to this insulin because it was made from pigs and not from humans. With GE, the gene that is responsible for making insulin in humans can be copied. It is put into bacteria or other organisms. The organisms produce the insulin, which is less likely to cause allergies because it comes from human genes instead of pigs.

Unnatural Versus Cheap and Nutritious

GE makes certain processes easier and less expensive. GE can also lead to more nutritious and better-tasting foods. According to the FDA, foods that come from scientifically engineered processes are as safe to eat as traditional foods. Some consumers and scientists are opposed to genetically engineered foods because they are unnatural. They claim that no one knows what the effects of eating these foods are and what unknown interactions might occur in people who eat the genetically engineered organisms. These concerns can be addressed only by further research, invention, and testing of GE products. The U.S. Department of Agriculture shows that more than seven thousand tests on new GE foods are currently under way.

Meanwhile, GE can provide solutions to food concerns and problems. In the early 1990s, tomato lovers complained about the tomatoes that were offered during off-seasons. The tomatoes were tasteless and hard. This complaint led to the first whole GE product to be put on the U.S. market in 1994. It was the Flavr Savr tomato. It was engineered to stay on the vine longer and to stay fresh longer while being shipped. It was also engineered for great taste. The company that made this GE tomato was Calgene. Calgene's research showed the FDA that Flavr Savr tomatoes were as safe as tomatoes found in nature. The FDA allowed the Flavr Savr on

Genetic engineering doesn't apply only to the things we eat and the medicines we need. It is also used in other processes, such as laundry. Many detergents contain genetically engineered enzymes. These enzymes make it possible to do different things while laundering clothes. Some GE enzymes allow clothes to be washed at room temperature. The clothes will get clean without scorching-hot water temperatures. Some enzymes are engineered to protect the clothes while they undergo the laundry cycle. Some enzymes are engineered to stop dyes from leaving fabrics, and some are engineered to protect fabrics from runaway dyes.

the market. The consumers who bought the tomatoes noticed the improvement over the tomatoes regularly offered during off-seasons. Although the Flavr Savr did solve the problem of off-season tomatoes, Calgene stopped making the tomato a few years later because of marketing, production, and other problems.

The genetic engineering of foods is a new field. No one, neither the scientists nor the consumers, knows all of the answers. The future of GE foods is still to be decided by the scientists and consumers who understand the issues. You're becoming one of the consumers who understands the issues . . . what do you think?

CHAPTER 2

NATURE VERSUS THE LABORATORY

Genetic engineering creates an unlimited number of possibilities because genes from any organism can be transferred to any other organism. Some plants produce toxic chemicals in their leaves so pests won't eat them. Using genetic engineering, scientists can transfer a toxin-producing gene to a potato plant. The potato plant then produces the toxin, and as a result, the pests won't eat it. This is an example of what genetic engineering can do but that selective breeding can never do.

Selective Breeding

Traditional breeding of crops and animals works with traits that appear in the gene pool of the organism. Genes are transferred from parents to offspring through sexual reproduction. Organisms with the desired traits are bred, and hopefully, the traits are passed on to the offspring. This process is slow. In both plants and animals, it may take

People have domesticated plants and animals to adapt to their needs.

many years to effectively breed the specific traits that are desired. In plants, it may take several growing seasons for the trait to become established. In some plants, such as trees, it may take decades before the success or failure of selective breeding becomes apparent.

Grafting

One of the early applications of science to traditional breeding was used in plants. This process—known as grafting—can be traced back about four thousand years to China and Mesopotamia. In grafting, the upper part of a plant is attached to the root system of another plant. While this process is still used today, it is not as simple as it sounds. Not every plant can be grafted to another plant. However, when it does work, the grafted plant can have the advantages of both plants.

For example, a certain variety of apple tree may be well suited for growing in a particular climate, but its fruits may be susceptible to disease. The roots and trunk of that tree could be used, and the branches of a disease-resistant apple tree could be grafted on. This provides an apple tree that is suited for its environment and fruit that is resistant to disease. The problem with this method is that these desired characteristics will not be passed on to the tree's offspring.

Seedless Fruits

In the 1970s and 1980s, farmers began growing seedless fruits, such as oranges, grapes, and watermelons. These seedless fruits are not really seedless, but they don't produce a large amount of seeds. Seedless fruits are more accurately called triploid fruits. Normal plants have two sets of chromosomes. Plants and animals with two sets of chromosomes are called diploid.

It can take many generations for a trait to become established.

When plants and animals reproduce, each parent passes a copy of one set of chromosomes to the offspring. This means that the offspring has two sets of chromosomes, one from each parent. Plants that produce seedless fruits have three sets of chromosomes. Having three sets of chromosomes is called triploid. These plants do not have the correct number of chromosomes and are mostly sterile because they produce very few seeds. The offspring grown from those few seeds are triploid and also will produce the seedless fruit.

Seedless fruit is popular with consumers because it is convenient to eat. The lack of seeds means that less time is spent picking out seeds and more time is spent enjoying the fruit. Watermelons are a popular seedless fruit. If you have ever seen a non-seedless watermelon cut in half, you have seen that the red, juicy flesh has many rows of black mature seeds and white immature seeds. Seedless watermelons have about 99.9 percent fewer seeds.

The original seedless fruits from the 1970s and 1980s were the result of breeding. However, in the late 1990s, scientists learned how to insert two genes into eggplant that caused the now transgenic eggplant to stop producing seeds. It was also found that the flowers didn't need to be fertilized for the fruit to form. This meant that the fruit could form in conditions in which normal fruit could not. Because the resulting plants are completely sterile, there is no way that they can reproduce.

To make more plants, scientists have to insert genes into fertile seeds each time they want to grow seedless fruits. Although this technology was tested on eggplant, scientists are fairly certain that these procedures can be used on just about any fruit or vegetable plant.

Gene manipulation helps fruits last longer in the market.

Methods of Genetic Engineering

Genetic engineering is a broad term that refers to a number of different methods of manipulating genes. The most common methods are genetic manipulation, recombinant DNA, targeted genetics, and, in humans, gene therapy. In agricultural crop and animal development, the most common methods are genetic manipulation and recombinant DNA.

Genetic manipulation involves turning on (activating) or turning off (deactivating) genes that already exist in an organism. The Flavr Savr tomato is an example of gene manipulation. To make the tomato, scientists turned off the gene that causes tomatoes to soften when they are ripe.

Recombinant DNA occurs when scientists insert a gene from one organism into another, creating a transgenic organism. The bacteria taken from the calf's gene that ultimately produced rennin was created with recombinant DNA.

Gene manipulation has limits similar to those of selective breeding. Scientists can work only with genes that an organism already has. Unlike selective breeding, scientists can more readily control the genes, and the desired results are obtained in a short time. Selective breeding may take years or decades before the desired results are obtained. Genetic manipulation can lead to the desired result immediately.

Recombinant DNA

Recombinant DNA is a technique whereby genes from a different organism—even a different species—are inserted into another organism. The new organism—a transgenic organism—has some new characteristics due to the inserted gene. The DNA of an organism acts like a blueprint that tells the cells how to make proteins. Proteins are the building blocks of an organism.

DNA is a long chain of molecules linked together in the shape of a double helix. The easiest way to picture a double helix is to picture a ladder. The side rails of the ladder are strings of large molecules linked together. The steps of the ladder are bonds between the large molecules. To make DNA more compact, the molecules are twisted.

When the cell is ready to make a protein, the DNA molecule separates at the bonds between the strands. A short section of the DNA is then copied, and the copy is transferred to a ribosome. The ribosome reads the instructions from the DNA copy and assembles a protein from amino acids in the cell. The amino acids in the cell are from digested food. Cells use this process to make all the proteins that are needed for the organism to survive.

When scientists insert a new segment of DNA into an organism's DNA, the organism then has instructions in its DNA to make a new protein. This new protein is assembled from all the same amino acids as in the original organism. This is the process by which bacteria can produce rennin the same way the cells of a calf's stomach do. Because the transgenic organism has the new instructions in its DNA, all of the offspring of the transgenic organism also have the same desired characteristic, and just as in gene manipulation, the results of recombinant DNA are immediate.

The process for making a transgenic organism is complicated but not technologically difficult. The first step is to identify an organism with the desired gene. This can be a plant, animal, or microorganism. Then the gene must be identified in the genetic sequence of the organism. When the DNA sequence is identified, it is cut out of the DNA with an enzyme. The DNA fragment for the gene, called a recombinant sequence, is then copied. Next, a copy of the recombinant sequence is inserted into

THE FIRST TRANSGENIC PLANTS

The first transgenic plants created were petunias and tobacco. These transgenic plants were developed in 1983. After that, scientists created transgenic potatoes and soybeans in 1987. In 1990, the first transgenic corn came from the laboratory. According to the U.S. Government Accounting Office

(GAO), the FDA had tested over fifty transgenic products as of April 2002. Most of these transgenic plants are types of corn, cotton, soybean, and sorghum. In addition, GE has created transgenic varieties of barley, beet, broccoli, cantaloupe, carrot, chicory, cranberry, eggplant, gladiolus, grape, papaya, pea, pepper, radish, raspberry, rice, squash, strawberry, sugarcane, sweet potato, watermelon, and wheat.

the DNA of another organism. This results in a transgenic organism that contains a new segment in its DNA. The transgenic organism is then allowed to multiply.

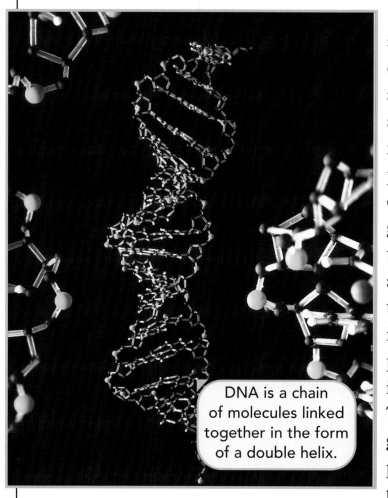

DNA is a chain of molecules linked together in the form of a double helix.

Scientists use a variety of different methods to accomplish the same results. The methods used on plant cells, animal cells, and microorganisms differ, but the end results are the same. The transgenic organism has a new piece of DNA in its original DNA. This new transgenic DNA is then passed on to all the offspring. This is what causes concern among some people about using transgenic organisms for food. No one really knows the long-term effects of adding DNA.

CHAPTER 3

WHY DO WE NEED GENETIC ENGINEERING?

On October 12, 1999, the United Nations declared that the population of the world was 6 billion. In 1987, the world population was 5 billion. In 1960, it was 3 billion. In 1900, the population of the world was just under 2 billion.

The United Nations predicts that by the year 2050, the world population will be about 9 billion. The rapidly expanding population of Earth is beginning to strain the resources of the planet. There are finite resources available for use. These resources include water, soil, and land area for crops.

Because of the rapidly growing population and the reduction in area for agriculture, more efficient means of producing food must be found. One answer to this concern is to create more efficient crops using genetic engineering. Genetically engineered crops can produce more food or higher quality food, be resistant to disease or climate, or grow in a shorter amount of time. As the population increases, these characteristics will become even more important. One of the goals of research into genetically engineered crops and animals is to provide quality food for the entire population of the world.

About 95 percent of the world's population live in poor, developing countries. Much of the terrain in these countries does not allow for the cultivation of land. We need to find ways to increase crop yields in areas where good soil and water are plentiful. Genetic engineering may be one way to accomplish this goal.

The Goals of Genetic Engineering

Scientists are focusing most research on two different aspects: insect resistance and herbicide resistance. Insects have plagued crops since the beginning of agriculture. Insects can destroy or greatly reduce crop yields. Farmers have traditionally used pesticides to kill insect pests. The problems with pesticides are numerous. Pesticides usually are not selective in the insects that they kill. This means that beneficial insects—the ones that help plants, such as ants that protect trees from other insects or predators that try to eat their leaves—are also killed by the pesticides.

Pesticides also usually do not break down quickly in the environment. This means that when it rains, runoff from the fields carries the pesticides into streams, rivers, and lakes. Pesticides can kill off many different kinds of organisms that live in these environments. Some pesticides are also toxic to humans. Farmers who spray their crops are exposed to the pesticides, as are consumers. Some pesticides are absorbed by plants and later eaten by consumers. Many people fear that pesticide residues can affect people by causing cancer or birth defects. By genetically engineering plants to resist insects, it is hoped that pesticide use by farmers can be greatly reduced. This could be a great benefit to the environment and people's health.

Insect-resistant crops are one of the goals of genetic engineering.

Another problem faced by farmers is weeds. A field with many weeds will have a lower yield because the crop must compete with the weeds for soil, nutrients, and sunlight.

Several herbicides are available that farmers can use to kill weeds. The problem is that the herbicides also kill or weaken the crop. This further reduces crop yields. Through genetic engineering, scientists have created crops that resist different herbicides. This allows farmers to use heavier applications of mild herbicides. If the crop is resistant to the effects of the herbicide, the weeds will be killed and the crop will flourish.

By using less powerful pesticides and herbicides, farmers cause fewer environmental problems. The end result is that farming becomes more profitable and less damaging to the environment. Farmers produce more food for less money. The savings can be passed on to consumers, and the world's increasing population benefits from a safer environment.

Food for a Growing World

Some see genetic engineering as a valuable tool to help feed the world's growing population. Genetic engineering has the potential of creating crops that will produce foods with higher nutritional value. Through genetic engineering, it may be possible to produce soybeans that contain additional proteins. The additional proteins would make for a more nutritious soybean. Another possibility is the engineering of plants that can survive harsh conditions, such as frost, drought, or extreme heat.

Herbicides and pesticides contaminate the soil and water.

Plants have certain temperature requirements for growing. A crop that normally grows in warm climates might be engineered to grow in cool climates. This would increase the number of potential areas where the plant could be grown. The same is true for plants that grow only in cool climates. If they could be engineered to live in warmer climates, then there would be more places where they could grow. Plants that are drought tolerant could survive on less water. This means that they could be grown in drier climates.

If water and fertilizers are used efficiently, more crops can be grown.

Any scientific engineering that increases the number of places a crop can grow will also increase the potential food supply.

CHAPTER 4

OUR HEALTH AND THE ENVIRONMENT

If transgenic organisms are used for food, they could have unknown effects on people. Even though the proteins produced by transgenic organisms are exactly the same as the proteins produced by the original organism, no one knows if other harmful interactions may occur.

Human Health

Are genetically engineered foods dangerous? While many scientists feel that genetically engineered foods are safe, there is a possibility that some are not. Scientists working in the field believe that because transgenic organisms are only producing proteins that already exist, they should be safe.

If a scientist adds a gene from a bacterium (the singular form of the word "bacteria") to a tomato, the tomato produces a protein that was produced in the original bacterium. Because there is no difference between the protein produced by the bacterium and the protein produced by the transgenic tomato, there should be no danger in eating the tomato. One of the greatest fears is that the new protein in the transgenic organism may cause some strange interactions.

Food allergies are one concern associated with the safety of transgenic organisms as food. In the United States, between 2.5 and 5 million people suffer from food allergies. According to the FDA, about 90 percent of all food allergies in the United States are caused by cows' milk, eggs, fish and shellfish, peanuts, soybeans, tree nuts, and wheat.

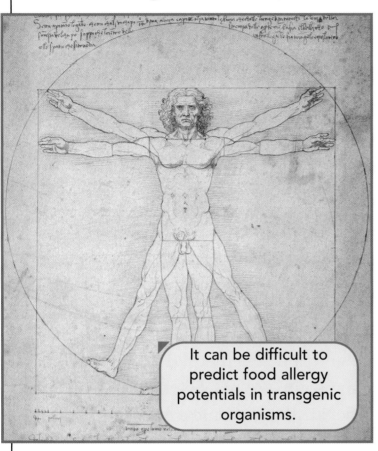

It can be difficult to predict food allergy potentials in transgenic organisms.

Allergic reactions can range from mild discomfort to life-threatening anaphylactic shock. Food allergies are poorly understood in humans, and some people are concerned that transgenic organisms could increase the number of food allergies. Due to the lack of information about the causes of food allergies, it is difficult to test food for allergy potentials. In some cases, food allergies do not show up until after repeated exposure or years of consumption.

The concern about food allergies is real. There have already been cases of transgenic organisms causing allergic reactions. In 1996, a transgenic soybean plant was created that included a gene from the Brazil nut. The result was a soybean with increased nutritional content. Researchers in Nebraska found that this transgenic soybean could cause serious allergies in people sensitive to Brazil nuts. Animal tests of the soybean had shown no allergens. Humans with Brazil nut allergies, however, did experience allergic reactions after trying the soybeans. Plans to grow and market that particular transgenic soybean plant were stopped.

Environmental Concerns

Some people fear that transgenic plants and animals pose problems for the environment. As we saw, one potential use for genetic engineering is to produce crops that resist herbicides, diseases, or pests. If successful, cultivation can be done using fewer or no pesticides. Reducing or eliminating pesticides could lower the cost of producing crops and make them safer. Some transgenic plants have been engineered to resist herbicides that are used to kill weeds. Killing weeds in fields makes crops grow better because they have less competition from other plants. In light of these positive benefits, how could the transgenic crops hurt the environment?

One possible effect is that crops could cross with native plants and pass along the transgenic genes. For example, wheat is a common crop and is closely related to some grasses. If transgenic wheat was developed that was resistant to herbicides and it crossed with a naturally occurring grass species, the offspring of the cross would contain the gene resistant to the herbicide. If this happened, the grass could then become a nuisance to wheat farmers. It would be a weed resistant to the herbicide used to remove it from fields. This could upset the balance of plant species in nearby native plant communities.

There has been little research done on how crops affect a given area's native plants. Transgenic crops offer an interesting opportunity for such studies because scientists often insert a DNA tag, or marker, to identify transgenic organisms.

Sorghum is another common crop that has been genetically engineered. In an effort to make sorghum farming more efficient, scientists added a gene to give the crop a resistance to Roundup, an herbicide. By giving the genetically engineered sorghum a resistance to Roundup, farmers can spray their fields with the herbicide to kill weeds. One of the weeds that plagues sorghum fields is Johnson grass. Johnson grass is closely related to sorghum; in fact, they are in the same genus. Scientists started looking at Johnson grass that grows in fields with the sorghum to see if there was any cross-pollination. They found that up to 12 percent of the Johnson grass in these fields and out to a distance of 100 meters (328 feet) from the fields shows the engineered gene from the sorghum. Scientists also know that the insects that pollinate the sorghum and Johnson grass routinely travel as much as 1 kilometer (.62 mile) to other fields. Even though the rate at which the genes are transferred is low, the Roundup-resistant Johnson grass genes will spread rapidly through the wild population.

Cross-pollination can spread genes in unpredictable ways.

There are many potential problems with genetically engineered crops. Some people fear that the spread of transgenic crops threatens natural crop diversity. Crops may lose their natural resistance to other diseases, which could lead to future problems. If transgenic plants pass resistance to herbicides to other plants, the other plants could become superweeds that are difficult or impossible to kill. Even if superweeds are not created, volunteer plants—offspring of the transgenic plants that sprout the following year—could become herbicide-resistant "weeds" if the fields are used for other crops. Transgenic plants could cause pests such as insects, bacteria, and viruses to become super pests that are difficult to kill or control. All of these potential problems could not only affect the crops and their pests but could also spell trouble for the entire ecosystem.

Consumers

How widespread is the use of genetically modified food in the United States? The answer is scary: No one really knows.

In 2002, it was estimated that about 71 percent of all cotton, 34 percent of all corn, and 75 percent of all soybeans grown in the United States were from transgenic plants. Each year, these numbers are rising. In 1992, the FDA started requiring the testing of all transgenic foods that contain genes from eggs, milk, wheat, shellfish, legumes (beans), and nuts. Foods in these groups make up about 90 percent of all known food allergies. The FDA also passed regulations requiring that transgenic foods made in America carry warning labels to alert the public.

The regulations requiring warning labels are difficult to enforce. The enforcement problem is further complicated by the fact that many processed foods contain soy or corn products. Soy protein is found in about 60 percent of processed foods, such as frozen dinners, baby foods, and yogurt. Corn is found in a wide variety of corn chips, tortillas, and cornstarch. Corn sweeteners are found in soda and fruit juices. With all of these products that use corn and soy, it is likely that they contain transgenic genes.

Another dilemma that some consumers face arises when animal genes are inserted into plants. There are many people who do not eat meat or animal products. Many vegetarian meat substitutes are made with soybeans. Tofu is also made from soybeans. Vegetarians need to know when soy products contain animal products.

Regulating Genetically Engineered Crops

The United States Department of Agriculture (USDA) is the federal agency that oversees issues concerning agriculture. The USDA is focusing on creating regulations that govern the rapidly growing field of genetic engineering of crops. The USDA determines the status of transgenic organisms based on their resemblance to the original organism. It then allows field-testing based on its determinations.

These rules allow the USDA to make rapid decisions about which transgenic organisms can be field-tested. These rules have shortened the time it takes for actual field trials to begin. Some argue that the USDA has too much power and that the short governmental review time could lead to mistakes. Others argue that giving the USDA the

No one really knows how widespread genetically modified food has become.

power to make quick decisions allows research to move forward quickly, as technology develops. In any case, the regulations allow the USDA to reduce paperwork and make field trials happen more quickly.

Labeling Transgenic Foods

While the USDA is responsible for ensuring that crops are safe to grow, the FDA is responsible for making sure that the crops are also safe to eat. Currently, there is no requirement for labeling foods as transgenic. In 2002, about 34 percent of the United States's corn crop (18 million acres) was grown with transgenic plants. For the soybean crop, about 75 percent (38 million acres) was transgenic, and more than one-third of the cotton crop (5 million acres) was transgenic. GE crop popularity is reaching the entire world as well. According to PBS, about 4 million acres worldwide were GE crops in 1996. According to the International Service for the Acquisition of Agri-biotech Applications (ISAAA), GE crops had reached more than 130 million acres worldwide by 2002. This means that imported products may also be transgenic, with little or no labeling. Currently, the only way to be sure that food products do not contain transgenic products is to select products that carry the organic label. Organic products are grown or raised in such a way that neither chemical pesticides nor transgenic materials are used.

CHAPTER 5

GENETIC ENGINEERING POSSIBILITIES

The recent *Jurassic Park* movies showed what might happen if dinosaurs were brought back to life with the help of genetic engineering. In the movies, the dinosaurs became uncontrollable. The realities of genetic engineering are much more benign. Genetic engineering is most easily performed on plants. It can be used to make crops resist pests, pesticides, and droughts, and become more nutritious. With genetic engineering, there are almost limitless possibilities.

Strange Foods

The goals of genetically engineering crops are to boost nutritional values or improve color, texture, shape, flavor, or other desired characteristics. To reach these goals, scientists insert some new genes into common crops.

You have already read about tomatoes that stay fresh and soybeans with extra nutritional value, but what else is possible? Freezing temperatures can quickly destroy crops in the field before they ripen or are harvested. The weather is beyond our control, so making crops resistant to cold is one solution. Scientists have removed a gene from an arctic flounder, which thrives in cold water. The gene was inserted into a tomato plant. The result is a tomato plant that can withstand colder temperatures.

Scientists have created wheat that has higher levels of gluten. The extra gluten makes breads that are lighter and fluffier. Scientists have engineered strawberries that have less sugar, so they taste more tart. Using genetic manipulation, scientists have developed coffee plants that actually grow decaffeinated coffee beans. Research has led to potatoes with extra starch, as well as beans and grains with extra protein.

Scientists also have the potential to make crops that let farmers know that they need watering or if pests or diseases are attacking. These "smart" crops could have genes from fireflies that cause the plant to start glowing when it becomes stressed either by pests or environmental factors.

Genetic Nightmares

Opponents of genetically engineered foods fear that transgenic crops may become monsters. These are not the kinds of monsters from the movies that attack cities and attempt to destroy our civilization. But some people have dubbed transgenic crops "Frankenfoods" in reference to Frankenstein's monster. They use past failed crop experiments, as well as recent examples of potential problems, to support their opinion.

In the 1960s, a variety of potato was developed through selective breeding. The variety showed resistance to insect

Genetic engineers see a future of disease-fighting foods. These foods would work to right whatever was wrong in our bodies on a regular basis.

- Vegetables with cancer-fighting chemicals
- Medical bananas that deliver vaccines
- Vegetable oils that fight heart disease
- Vegetables that provide a full meal's worth of proteins in one serving
- Coffee beans that don't contain caffeine

Some scientists also believe that GE could be used to right some of the wrongs we've done to our environment. One fantastical idea is a fish that eats and lives off of toxic or poisonous waste. This comes from the fact that some fish have undergone GE to have proteins that grab or soak up metal minerals. Can you think of any ideas that GE could be used for to better the environment?

pests. Unfortunately, the tubers—the edible part of potato plants—produced high levels of a toxin. The potatoes were unfit for consumption. Another unsuccessful selective breeding experiment took place in the 1980s. A new variety of celery was developed. This variety resisted many of the insect pests that attack the celery crop. Unfortunately, people who were handling the celery began having severe skin rashes. It was discovered that the celery was producing a chemical that caused rashes when it was exposed to sunlight.

These were examples of selective breeding techniques. What horror stories have happened with the genetic engineering of plants?

You have already read about allergic reactions to Brazil nut genes in soybeans. Another example of difficulties with

46

genetically engineered crops occurred when scientists tried to create crops that were resistant to insect pests. The corn borer is an insect that has serious effects on corn crops. Farmers use pesticides to control corn borers in their fields.

Genetic engineering brought a solution to the problem. Scientists inserted a gene from a bacterium, *Bacillus thuringiensis,* into corn plants. This created a corn plant that produced a chemical called Bt toxin. The Bt toxin kills corn borers that eat any part of the corn plant. The same gene has also been inserted into cotton and potato plants to protect them against pests as well. The Bt toxin was thought to kill the pests and not harm any beneficial insects.

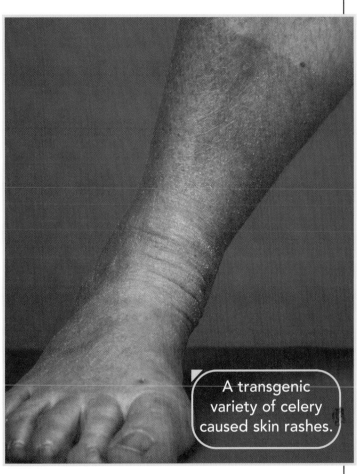

A transgenic variety of celery caused skin rashes.

A problem with the Bt toxin gene showed up in cotton plants. Not all cotton borers were killed by the Bt toxin. Some of the insects developed a resistance to it. These Bt toxin–resistant cotton borers passed the resistance gene on to their offspring. The result was that in some areas, crops were overrun by pests that were resistant to the genetically engineered toxin. The cotton borers decimated the crops, causing an extremely low yield. Scientists were not surprised by the insects' developing a resistance. This has been a problem with all pesticides that have been developed.

The Bt toxin gene in transgenic corn pollen unintentionally affected the monarch butterfly.

By 1998, almost 25 percent of the 80 million acres of corn planted in the United States had some form of the Bt toxin gene in it. Corn plants are wind pollinated. The plants produce tremendous quantities of pollen. The pollen coats everything near the cornfields. A 1999 study by Cornell University found that corn pollen containing the Bt toxin gene could kill monarch butterfly caterpillars. Monarch butterfly caterpillars eat only milkweed. Milkweed is often found growing in ditches and fields in corn-growing areas. When the transgenic corn pollen settled on the milkweed, monarch caterpillars ate the pollen along with the milkweed. Within days, they died. Scientists fear that it could be disastrous for monarch butterflies if more transgenic corn is planted.

Preventing Genetic Nightmares

Insects breed rapidly, and because of their numbers, they have a great genetic diversity. It is not unusual for insects to develop resistance to any pesticide, whether it is sprayed on the crops or inserted into the crop's genes. To combat this natural selection in insect breeding, scientists have suggested a planting strategy to reduce the problem.

First, farmers are asked to plant an area with a variety of the crop that does not have the engineered gene. One manufacturer requires that these areas be 20 percent of the entire area planted if they are sprayed with conventional pesticides or 4 percent if they are left unsprayed. The areas act as a refuge for the pest insects. That way, when the transgenic crop kills all but the resistant insects, the resistant insects breed with the normal population from the refuge. Because the insects in the refuge have normal genes, the gene for resistance is diluted in the gene pool of the pests. This means that the pests do not breed an entire population that is resistant.

As transgenic organisms are created, they must be studied before becoming available to consumers.

This practice began in the late 1980s. So far it has been relatively successful in preventing the spread of resistant pests. In Europe, these methods were not used. It was found that after only six or seven growing seasons, a majority of the European pests showed resistance. But scientists are not sure whether using islands of crops as refuges will work. They do not even agree on the size or proximity of these refuges. Estimates for the ideal size of the islands range from a small percentage up to 50 percent of the crop area. Further research is needed to determine what percentage should be used and whether it will actually be effective.

The Future of Genetic Engineering

Do transgenic crops make sense? Many farmers and seed companies think that they do. Farming supplies the world's population with food. As the population grows, the need for more efficient farming becomes more pressing. The use of transgenic crops may be a good solution to the problem.

Genetic engineering is a new technology. Just like any new technology, the potential uses and abuses need to be studied. Before transgenic organisms are used by or sold to consumers, they need to be carefully studied and used in controlled situations. Genetic engineering, like other new technologies, may enhance everyone's quality of life, but the enhancement may come at a cost.

CHAPTER 6

CONSUMERS AND GENETIC ENGINEERING

The future of genetically engineered foods may not be up to scientists. The final decision may rest with consumers. If genetically engineered foods are accepted, they will become more common. If consumers choose not to accept transgenic foods, their use may be limited or stopped altogether.

The Role of the FDA

The FDA first addressed the issue of transgenic foods in 1992. At that time, the FDA set forth its policy on transgenic foods. It requires that labeling on all foods be truthful and not misleading. It does not require that producers disclose information solely in response to consumers' desire for knowledge. The FDA does require that foods be given common or usual names. Also, the food label must disclose any information about possible consequences that may arise from the use of the product.

What does this ruling mean for transgenic foods? It means that genetically engineered foods need not have any special labeling in the United States. The only exceptions are cases in which the results of genetic engineering have significantly changed the food. For example, the labeling requirement concerns transgenic foods that may cause allergic reactions. If genes from peanuts were added to beans to increase the amount of protein, the transgenic beans would require special labeling because many people are allergic to peanuts.

Some people are concerned about transgenic foods and feel that they are not safe. They want transgenic foods

Consumers who wish to avoid transgenic foods should look for organic products.

to be labeled as such. Because there is no way of knowing whether a food is transgenic or contains transgenic products, the consumer has little choice. Consumers who wish to avoid transgenic foods should buy only foods that are labeled organic.

A Global Outlook

Labeling requirements vary in different countries around the world. In Europe, a recent poll showed that 40 percent of Europeans didn't believe scientists' claims that transgenic foods are safe. Also, 50 percent of Europeans polled said that food safety was their number one concern. As a result of public concerns, the European Union introduced labeling requirements. Some European supermarkets have labeled their brand-name products "GMO-free" (GE is also referred to as GMO, or genetically modified. In the United Kingdom, transgenic foods have been banned from 1,300 schools, and the government is considering banning the widespread growth of transgenic crops.

All over the world, the majority of people polled want genetically engineered foods labeled. In Canada, the use of a genetically engineered growth hormone for cows, developed by a U.S. company, was rejected. The Canadian government decided that there had not been enough studies to prove it was safe for humans to consume the milk. In Mexico and Latin America, citizens are calling for more research before transgenic crops are grown or sold to the public.

Japan, the largest producer of soybean products, decided to ban genetically engineered soybeans from all of its products. Other manufacturers are following its lead and are stopping the use of transgenic products. Even though the Japanese government has approved twenty-two transgenic varieties of six crops—soybean, corn, canola, potato, cotton, and tomato—it has also decided to impose strict labeling requirements. The labeling gives Japanese consumers a choice about what they eat.

Public Perceptions and Acceptance

To make informed decisions about whether genetically engineered foods are safe, people need to be educated about the issues involved. Additional information can be found through local and national news, newspapers, magazines, and various Web sites. Because genetic engineering is a new technology and a rapidly advancing field, the types of crops and the issues involved are constantly changing. The next time you eat a tomato (or anything else), ask yourself where it came from.

GLOSSARY

anaphylactic shock Hypersensitivity to a foreign substance; severe allergic reaction.

Bacillus thuringiensis Naturally-occurring bacterium that lives in soil and on plants and produces a protein that is toxic to insects. This protein can be inserted into plants to create Bt toxin and make them resistant to insects.

chromosome DNA-containing structure found in the nucleus of a cell.

diploid Normal condition of DNA in cells where genetic information exists in pairs.

diversity Measurement of the number of different species in a habitat.

DNA (deoxyribonucleic acid) Molecule that stores all the genetic information for an organism.

enzyme Protein that is an important part of biochemical reactions in cells.

Food and Drug Administration (FDA) U.S. government organization that is responsible for food safety.

GLOSSARY

Frankenfoods Term used to describe genetically altered food, alluding to Frankenstein's monster, who was built from many different parts.

gene Specific segment of DNA that is responsible for exhibiting a trait.

gene manipulation Rearrangement of DNA to achieve a new and desirable effect.

genetic engineering Manipulating, inserting, or removing genetic material from an organism to create desired results.

grafting Union of parts from two different plants.

herbicide Substance used to kill plants.

organic pesticides Substances used to kill pests that are made up of carbon-containing chemical compounds.

recombinant DNA Genetic engineering method in which a gene is inserted into the genetic material of another organism.

selective breeding Breeding process in which organisms with certain traits are crossed with other organisms with specific traits in hopes that the same traits show up in the offspring.

transgenic organism Genetically modified organism.

triploid Organism with an extra set of chromosomes in addition to the normal pairs.

FOR MORE INFORMATION

In the United States

Campaign for Food Safety/Organic Consumers Association
6101 Cliff Estate Road
Little Marais, MN 55614
(218) 226-4164
Web site: http://www.purefood.org/gelink.html

Council for Responsible Genetics
5 Upland Road, Suite 3
Cambridge, MA 02140
(617) 868-0870
Web site: http://www.gene-watch.org

National Institutes of Health (NIH)
National Center for Biotechnology Information
U.S. National Library of Medicine
8600 Rockville Pike
Bethesda, MD 20894
Web site: http://www.ncbi.nlm.nih.gov

FOR MORE INFORMATION

In Canada

Canadian Food Inspection Agency, Office of Biotechnology
59 Camelot Drive
Ottawa, ON K1A 0Y9
(613) 225-2342

Canadian Partnership for Consumer Food Safety Education
Suite 161-75 Alberta Street
Ottowa, ON KIP 5E7
(613) 798-3042
e-mail: fightbac@canfightbac.org

Web Sites

Due to the changing nature of Internet links, the Rosen Publishing Group, Inc., has developed an online list of Web sites related to the subject of this book. This site is updated regularly. Please use this link to access the list:

http://www.rosenlinks.com/fss/scef

FOR FURTHER READING

Bailey, Britt, and Marc Lappe. *Against the Grain: Biotechnology and the Corporate Takeover of Your Food.* Monroe, ME: Common Courage Press, 1998.

Bains, William. *Biotechnology from A to Z.* Oxford, UK: Oxford University Press, 1998.

Cefrey, Holly. *Cloning and Genetic Engineering.* New York: Scholastic Library Publishing, 2001.

Judson, Karen. *Genetic Engineering: Debating the Benefits and Concerns.* Berkeley Heights, NJ: Enslow Publishers, Incorporated, 2001.

Marshall, Elizabeth L. *High-Tech Harvest: A Look at Genetically Engineered Foods.* Danbury, CT: Franklin Watts, 1999.

Silver, Lee M. *Remaking Eden: How Genetic Engineering and Cloning Will Transform the American Family.* New York: Avon Books, 1998.

Torr, James D. *Genetic Engineering.* Farmington Hills, MI: Gale Group, 2000.

Yount, Lisa. *The Ethics of Genetic Engineering.* Farmington Hills, MI: Gale Group, 2001.

BIBLIOGRAPHY

"Are Bioengineered Foods Safe?" Food and Drug Administration (December 1999). Retrieved October 15, 2002 (http://www.fda.gov/fdac/features/2000/100_bio.html).

Cummins, Ronnie. *Hazards of Genetically Engineered Foods and Crops.* Little Marais, MN: Organic Consumers Association, 2001.

"Engineer a Crop." PBS.org. Retrieved October 15, 2002 (http://www.pbs.org/wgbh/harvest).

"Genetically Engineered Food Safety Problems—An Impartial Evaluation." Physicians and Scientists for Responsible Application of Science and Technology. Retrieved October 15, 2002 (http://www.psrast.org/indexeng.htm).

"Harvest of Fear." *Nova* and *Frontline*, PBS (2001).

"Should We Grow GM Crops?" PBS.org. Retrieved October 15, 2002 (http://www.pbs.org/wgbh/harvest).

INDEX

INDEX

CREDITS

About the Author

Allan B. Cobb is a freelance science writer who lives in central Texas. He has written books, articles, radio scripts, and educational materials concerning different aspects of science. When not writing about science, he enjoys traveling, camping, hiking, and exploring caves.

Photo Credits

Designer: Mike Caroleo; Editor: Mark Beyer